Studies and Melodious Etudes for Alto Saxophone

by
Willis Coggins
in collaboration with
James Ployhar

To the Teacher

"Studies And Melodious Etudes", Level II, is a supplementary technic book of the Belwin "STUDENT INSTRUMENTAL COURSE". Although planned as a companion and correlating book to the method, "The Alto Saxophone Student", it can also be used effectively with most intermediate alto saxophone instruction books. It provides for extended and additional treatment in technical areas, which are limited in the basic method because of lack of space. Emphasis is on developing musicianship through scales, warm-ups and technical drills, musicianship studies and interesting melody-like etudes.

The Belwin "STUDENT INSTRUMENTAL COURSE" - A course for individual and class instruction of LIKE instruments, at three levels, for all band instruments.

EACH BOOK IS COMPLETE IN ITSELF BUT ALL BOOKS ARE CORRELATED WITH EACH OTHER

METHOD
"The Alto Saxophone Student"
For individual
or
class instruction

ALTHOUGH EACH BOOK CAN BE USED SEPARATELY, IDEALLY, ALL SUPPLEMENTARY BOOKS SHOULD BE USED AS COMPANION BOOKS WITH THE METHOD

STUDIES & MELODIOUS ETUDES	TUNES FOR TECHNIC	ALTO SAXOPHONE SOLOS	DUETS FOR STUDENTS

Supplementary scales, warm-up and technical drills, musicianship studies and melody-like etudes, all carefully correlated with the method.	Technical type melodies, variations, and "famous passages" from musical literature for the development of — technical dexterity.	Four separate correlated Solos, with piano accompaniment, written or arranged by Willis Coggins:
		
		To a Wild Rose . . *MacDowell*
		Aria . . . . *Coggins*
		Berceuse . . . . *Ilyinsky*
		Gavotte . . . . *Gluck*
			A book of carefully correlated duet arrangements of interesting and familiar melodies without piano accompaniments.
			Available for: Flute
			            B♭ Clarinet
			            Alto Sax
			            B♭ Cornet
			            Trombone

SAXOPHONE FINGERING CHART

How To Read The Chart

● - Indicates hole closed or keys to be pressed.

O - Indicates hole open.

When a number is given, refer to the picture of the Saxophone for additional keys to be pressed.

When two ways to finger a note are given, the first way is the one most often used. The second fingering is for use in special situations.

When two notes are given together (F♯ and G♭) they are the same tone and, of course, played the same way.

Etude No. 1

C Major Scale

Use Chromatic F♯ Fingering.   Use Regular F♯ Fingering.

Also play without slurs.

Etude No. 2

Allegro

F Major Scale

8th Note Abbreviations

Same: * *(See note below)*

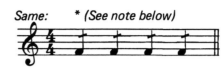

Same:

8th Note Abbreviations, with staccato marks.

Etude No. 3

Allegro

*A Bar across the stem means divide the note into Eighth notes. If staccato marks are added, play staccato 8th notes.

6

same

16th Note Abbreviations

Same: *(See note below)   Same:

16th Note Abbreviations, with staccato marks.

simile

simile

Etude No. 4

Moderato

mf

simile

* *TWO BARS across a stem means divide the note into sixteenth notes. If staccato marks are added, play staccato 16th notes.*

High Register Studies

Etude No. 5

8

Dotted Eighth Notes

Etude No. 6

.I.C.232

Counting Study

Syncopation Studies

A Syncopated Canon

Etude No. 7

*When 1st player arrives at third measure, second player starts at the beginning.

B.I.C.232

Review of B♭ Fingerings

Synocopation in ¾ Time.

Etude No. 8

Moderato

High Register Studies

D Major Scale

Slow and Fast § Time

Count: 1 2 3 4 5 6
Count: 1   2

Comparing ⅔ with Fast §

Count: 1 2   1 2   1 2   1 2

Fast §

Count   1   2

Etude No. 10

Moderato (in 2)

mf

Syncopation in ¢ Time

simile

Dotted Notes in 𝄵 and ¢ Time

Etude No. 11

Allegro

a minor Scale *(Natural)*   *(Harmonic)*

(Melodic)   Arpeggio

Fast

Also play :   etc.

Etude No. 12
Andantino (in 2)

d minor *(Natural)*

(Harmonic)

(Melodic)

Fast 6/8

Count: 1   2   1   2   etc.

Fast 6/8

Count: 1   2   1   2   etc.

Etude No. 13

A Minor

Andantino

e minor *(Natural)*   *(Harmonic)*

(Melodic)

Also play:

etc.

simile

Etude No. 14

D Minor

Moderato

f

rit

Etude No. 15

Etude for B♭ Fingering (No. 1)

18

Bb Major Scale

Grace Note Studies

*(Grace note)

Etude No. 16

E Minor

Moderato

f

* Play lightly, just before the main or accented note.

Fast **6/8**

Eighth Note Triplets

Count: 1   2   etc.

Count: 1   2   etc.

Etude No. 17

A Minor

Andante

mf

rit.

Quarter Note Triplets

Count: 1   2   etc.

Count: 1   2   etc.

Etude No. 18

Waltz tempo

Etude for B♭ Fingering (No. 3)

Fast

(abbreviation)

Fast

Staccato

Etude No. 19

Andantino (in 2)

Left Little Finger Studies

Slide the finger. Press firmly.

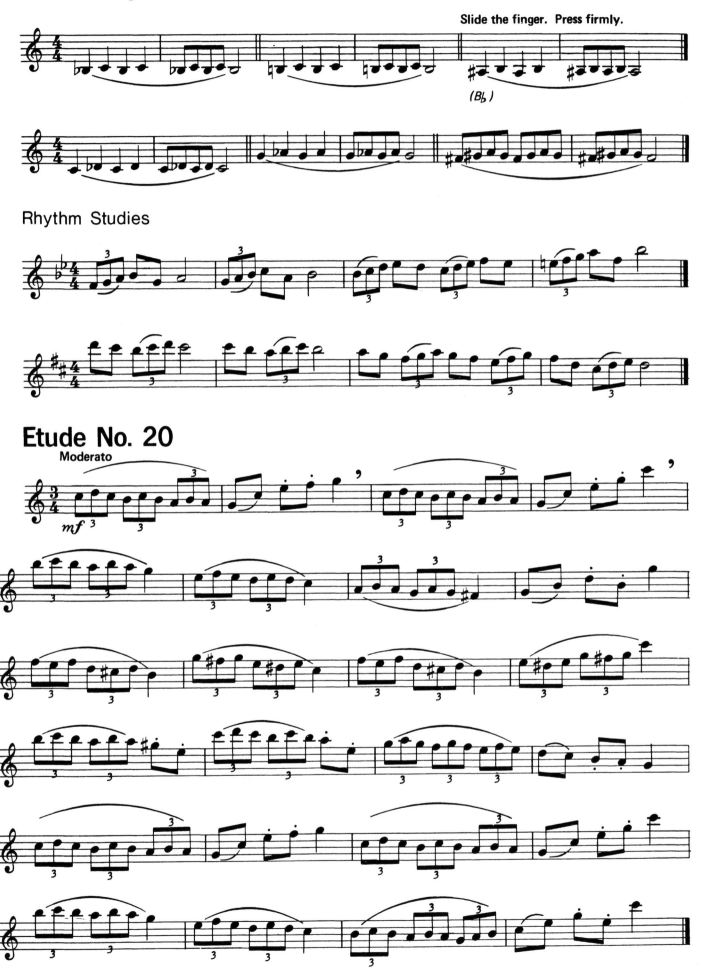

(B♭)

Rhythm Studies

Etude No. 20

Moderato

mf

Slide little finger. Press firmly.

b minor *(Natural)*   *(Harmonic)*

(Melodic)

Etude No. 21

Moderato

g minor *(Natural)*

(Harmonic)

(Melodic)

Arpeggio

Use Key 7

Use Key 5

Use Key 6

Etude No. 22

B Minor Etude

Allegro

A Major

Etude No. 23

G Minor Etude

Allegretto

Also play:

etc.

Practice slowly, then try for speed.
Play 3 times

End

Play 3 times

End

Etude No. 24

Allegro

Etude No. 25

28

c minor *(Natural)* *(Harmonic)*

(Melodic)

Right Little Finger Studies

(Slide little finger)

Etude No. 26
Moderato Etude for B♭ Fingering (No. 2)

E Major

Etude No. 27

Andantino

Etude No. 28

c# minor (Natural)   (Harmonic)

Like C♮

(Melodic)

Right Little Finger Studies

Keep Key 7 open

Keep Key 7 open

Etude No. 29
Moderato   F# Minor

f

p   (F♮)   *mf*

f

f   *p*

f

32

Etude No. 30

B.I.C.232